Campus Security *and* Crime Prevention

Compiled by

ASIS Standing Committee on Educational Institutions

ISBN 1-887056-08-4

Printed in the United States of America
10 9 8 7 6 5 4 3 2

TABLE OF CONTENTS

INTRODUCTION

Educational institutions throughout the world must ensure the safety and security of increasingly large numbers of students, faculty, and staff. A safe and secure campus enhances the atmosphere of learning desired in a collegiate setting, and encourages the support of the academic community. The return on investment is tangible, since both students and the general public are attracted to classes and events held in a safe and secure environment.

To ensure that campuses stay secure, administrators, along with their safety and security department personnel, must design, develop, and implement a strategic plan that details proactive ways to prevent crimes and protect assets at institutions of higher learning. Through this process, administrators will gain insight into the value of a viable safety and security department and be in a position to support the mission, goals, and objectives at the core of the strategic plan.

This book can serve as a resource for college and university administrators as well as for others involved in the pursuit of this specialty within the field of industrial security. The authors explore such topics as the legal aspects of campus security and the appropriate programs and equipment that help meet those requirements. Personnel factors are addressed as well, underscoring the need for diversity that provides for a culturally enriched campus.

The authors especially thank E. Floyd Phelps, CPP, 1997 chairman of the ASIS Standing Committee on Educational Institutions, for his efforts in guiding this book from a mere idea to a reality.

Linda M. Kinczkowski, Ph.D., Editor
Consultant

The Security Survey: An Essential Element in any Protective Plan

by Bruce D. Harman, CPP

How vulnerable is your campus? Do you know what your security and safety exposures are? Have you identified the possible targets on your campus? Do you know how, when, and where your losses are occurring? What are your plans to address these risks?

Most professional campus security officials have a good idea of what their exposures are and may even have developed an action plan to address them. Regrettably, a few, either by omission or commission, have failed to identify where their exposures lie.

In the *Protection of Assets Manual* published by Merritt, authors Healy and Walsh assert that "no security program can be effective unless it is based upon a clear understanding of the actual risks it is designed to control. Until the actual threats to assets is assessed accurately, precautions and countermeasures, even those of the highest quality, reliability, and repute, cannot be chosen except by guesswork."

The vulnerability assessment or security survey remains one of the best methods to assess the exposures germane to any protection plan or program. While most campus security directors may have examined their exposures, a review alone is not enough when a problem arises.

It is crucial for the campus security department to have an articulated assessment of the exposures on their campus and a plan to address them. We live in a very litigation-prone society. One of the worst situations could be for a court or the campus community to discover that a college or university has not made an effort to calculate campus vulnerabilities or has not fully recognized the risks arising from previous litigation or incidents against similar institutions. Institutions in that situation can rightly be considered negligent for failing to implement reasonable improvements.

This back to basics" approach is founded on solid ground. In the medical field, one of the first steps a physician takes when seeing a new patient is to learn the patient's medical history and conduct a physical. In light of that background, the physician can assess the current status of the patient's health.

The security survey accomplishes the same goal: it is a history and physical of the campus. Specifically, the professional conducting the security survey can ascertain the present security status, identify deficiencies, determine the protection needed, and recommend improvements to the overall security.

By conducting a security survey, security professionals document any loss prevention exposures, thereby placing the administration on notice of their concerns. Additionally, they can make recommendations to address these issues. While some of the recommendations may not be implemented for various reasons, the security department has insulated themselves from charges of negligence. This information may also serve as the basis for training programs and crime prevention awareness programs, supply justifications for capital budget expenditures, identify goals and objectives for the department, and result in changes to policies and procedures as well as staffing.

Conducting a Security Survey. Typically, a security survey includes the following four stages: assets definition, threat assessment, vulnerability analysis, and loss prevention recommendations.

In the *assets definition* stage, the analysis seeks to identify the college's assets and classify them in some sort of rank order. Generally, the survey team conducts this analysis building by building or department by department. The most important assets can be identified through interviews and a review of the campus-wide property inventory.

In the *threat assessment* stage, the survey team can explore the various ways in which the identified assets, be they personnel or property, can be threatened. Threats can be criminal, natural, accidental, and procedural. The assessment must seek to identify prior, existing, and future exposures to the various types of threats.

The historical records of the campus community will assist in identifying the past loss experiences of the community. Insurance claims, crime analysis reports, uniform crime statistics, safety committee minutes, and other relevant reports must be reviewed.

After examining all of the available information on past occurrences and identifying new risk exposures, the survey team moves to the *vulnerability analysis* stage of the survey. The team seeks first to determine the probability that any given event will occur. Next, the team must attempt to identify how critical that event might be and what effect its occurrence would have on the campus community. Each threat should be ranked according to some agreed-upon scale for both probability and criticality.

For example, a one could mean the threat was highly probable, in fact, virtually certain to occur; a two could mean it was probable; and a three could mean it was possible, but unlikely to occur. If the probability of occurrence was unknown, the team could give the threat a four.

Similarly, if the team labeled a threat as an A, it would mean that threat would be fatal to operations; if given a B, it would very seriously disrupt operations; if given a C, the disruption would be moderately serious; and a D would mean the effect on operations would be relatively unimportant. Those events where the seriousness was unknown could be labeled an E.

These rankings are important because those threats that are most likely to occur and will affect the most critical assets should receive first consideration when allocating loss prevention resources and setting up a time table for implementation.

In the last stage, appropriate *loss prevention recommendations* are made to include physical security measures such as alarms, locks, cameras, and fences; personnel security tactics such as adding officers or training staff; and policy or procedural changes. The most important aspect of these measures is that they must be integrated into a system. It would be pointless to install locks and intercoms on doors that the staff insists on leaving open.

The recommendations must be well thought out, prudent, reasonable, and cost-effective—a measured response to an identified problem. Needless to say, not all recommendations will be implemented immediately because of budgetary restrictions. Realistically, they will be phased in over time or even placed on hold. But still, the fact that the risks have been identified and recommendations set forth is pivotal to the process.

Survey Presentation. When completed, the survey results must be presented in a professional way, using the following seven major categories: executive summary, introduction, scope, findings, conclusions, recommendations, and attachments. This format will help those who review it to more easily comprehend its findings.

Losses occur for three reasons: failure to recognize vulnerabilities, failure to use the right countermeasures, or failure to consider change. The campus security professional should use the security survey as a way to assess the current posture of the organization's loss prevention capabilities. Admittedly, a professionally completed survey requires a substantial investment in time initially and a continuing commitment to keep the document updated and relevant. However, these activities yield high returns on investment and are crucial to the development of a comprehensive campus security program.

About the Author: Bruce D. Harman is a Certified Protection Professional and Director of Public Safety at New Jersey City University, Jersey City, New Jersey. He received a Bachelor of Science in Public Safety Administration from William Paterson College and a Master of Arts from Kean College, also of New Jersey.

Risk Management for Campus Administrators

by Bertus R. Ferreira, Ed.D., CPP

Risk management techniques have been used effectively for many years in business and industrial settings. College and university campuses face many of the same safety and security concerns and risks as their private sector counterparts. Risks are everywhere, and if not managed, they will cause many problems. Campus administrators must either do something about these risks, or be ready to answer to the courts when held liable.

The potential risks at educational institutions are numerous and very complicated. If a student or faculty member is assaulted, robbed, or raped, the institution can be held liable and may have to pay an enormous sum in litigation or an out-of-court settlement. If a certain campus is perceived as unsafe, students will take their tuition money elsewhere, a condition most educational institutions can ill afford. Colleges and universities house expensive equipment that can be stolen or damaged, such as computers, electronic appliances, laboratory equipment, art pieces, rare documents, and books. Replacement costs for any one of these items can be astronomical. All of these safety and security risks need attention.

Definitions. Before embarking on a preventive security program to address these specific issues, the university must decide what it valuesbe it people, property, or informationand to what degree it is willing to protect those valuables. This process can be completed using the following proven techniques.

Risk management comprises deliberate actions that anticipate, recognize, and analyze potential threats and losses. These actions include reducing or preventing such risks and evaluating the effectiveness of the measures taken.

Risk analysis includes examining the vulnerability, probability, and criticality of potential threats, including natural risks and man-made risks.

Natural risks include such calamities as earthquakes, floods, tornadoes, hurricanes and fires caused by lightning. These incidents are hard to predict, and even when we can, little can be done to prevent them from happening. The best safeguard is to reduce the consequences by controlling the damage that will occur. Preparing plans that include emergency responses, evacuation procedures, and repair services can help mitigate the extreme uncertainty that follows a natural disaster.

Man-made risks involve the actions of humans, including murder, rape, assault and battery, theft, and vandalism. Should one of these conditions occur, plans must consider the motivation, potential, capability, and opportunity for a person to commit such an act, thereby creating an unanticipated loss.

Vulnerability assessments recognize and identify the threats that may result in losses.

Educational institutions must recognize how vulnerable they are to various risks. Colleges are open to the general public, and the population reflects society in general with all its permutations. Access control is almost impossible on large campuses. Universities are often involved with controversial issues which are protected under academic freedom of speech. A certain political or social agenda may attract very emotional or radical people to the campus, which in turn may lead to the destruction of property and even riots.

Probability refers to the chance or likelihood that an incident or loss will take place.

It is indicated by a mathematical statement concerning the possibility of an event occurring and can be described by the formula indicated in **Exhibit 1**.

EXHIBIT 1.

Probability Formula

$$0 < P < 1$$

The probability, "P," is always larger than zero (no event occurs) but smaller than one (event occurs). The probability is either known or unknown. If it is known then the following scale can be applied:

0.999	**Virtually Certain**
0.75	**Very Probable**
0.50	**Average Probability**
0.25	**Less probable**
0.001	**Very improbable**

Criticality measures the impact of a loss in financial terms. The resulting calculation reflects how important the potential loss is in terms of the survival or existence of the institution and can be expressed using the scale shown in **Exhibit 2**. Once the consequences are known, effective plans can be developed to deal with them. Criticality calculations usually include the cost considerations listed in **Exhibit 3**.

Once the probability and criticality of certain risks have been determined, a decision must be made on how to handle them. The matrix in **Exhibit 4** can help in that process. If the risk is both very probable and very critical, then we will have to take swift action. If the risk is less critical and not very probable, we can wait or take a less drastic course of action.

Risk Management Alternatives and Strategies. A number of risk management strategies can be used to manage risks. Depending on where the risk falls on the probability and criticality matrix, institutions should use the following strategies:

Risk avoidance eliminates the risk by removing it altogether. If at all possible, problems should simply be removed from the campus. If a very busy street runs right through campus and the vehicles

EXHIBIT 2
Criticality Risks

The criticality of risks can be expressed as a percent, using the following scale:

100 percent – Fatal
75 percent – Very Serious
50 percent – Average
25 percent – Less Serious
0 percent – Unimportant

EXHIBIT 3
Cost Considerations for Criticality Calculations

The cost of the item lost.

The replacement cost of the item lost, including the new purchase price, the delivery cost, the installation cost, and indirect costs.

The cost of temporary replacements, if necessary.

Down time or the period during which the institution cannot function properly to fulfill its obligations to students and the community.

Discounted cash. If cash is urgently needed and must be withdrawn from savings early, penalties and lost interest will apply.

Insurance rate changes. Every time an insurance claim is filed the insurance company will recalculate the risk factors of the institution making the claim. As soon as they perceive the institution as more risk prone than previously thought, insurance rates will increase.

Loss of marketplace advantage. If an incident causes students to perceive that a specific campus environment is unsafe, they will go somewhere else for their education. An institution may need years to repair its reputation.

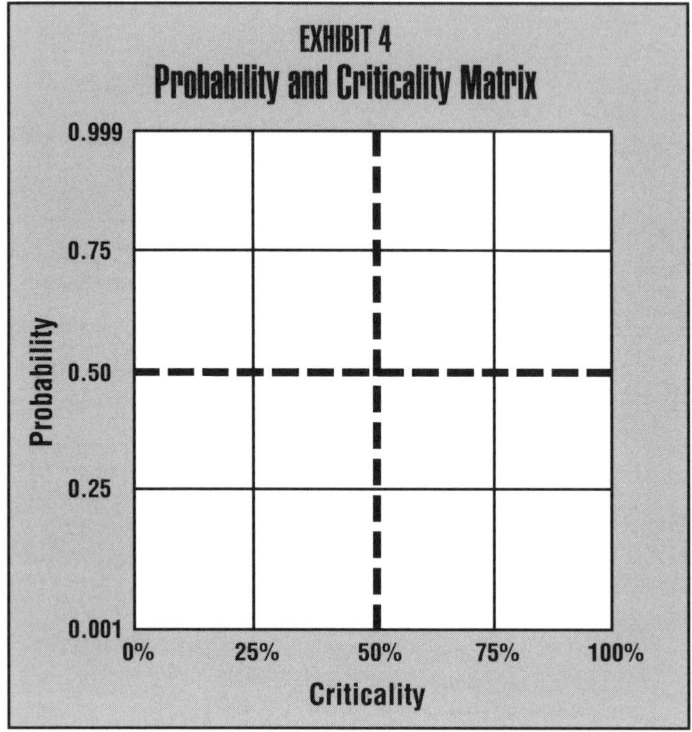

pose an unacceptable risk to students, the street can simply be closed. If the institution has a nuclear, biological, or chemical facility that has a high risk potential, it might be in the long-term interest of the university to close that facility down before an accident happens.

Risk avoidance is commonly implemented when an incident that could be caused by the risk would have catastrophic consequences to the institution, for example, if human life is endangered and the potential for devastating lawsuits is great. Whenever both the probability and criticality values are high when an incident is plotted on the matrix, risk avoidance should be considered immediately.

Risk reduction decreases the risk by minimizing the probability that the potential loss will occur. This reduction of criminal opportunity is often accomplished by situational crime prevention strategies to discourage, deter, or deny criminal incidents.

For example, if the campus has areas that are not well lit, adding more and better lighting will reduce the chance of criminals hiding in dark spots. Keeping doors locked after hours will deny access to criminals, thereby reducing the possible theft of equipment. Making students and faculty more aware of crime prevention strategies will make them less of a target.

Risk reduction strategies are often applied when the probability of an incident is high but the criticality to the institution is relatively low. By reducing the probability that something bad will happen, the institutions exposure to crime is limited.

Risk Spreading limits the effect of a potential loss through compartmentalization or decentralization. Fire prevention and control can be used as an example. If large quantities of flammable liquid or other dangerous material must be stored on campus, then it is best to store such high risk items in a separate building. Then, if they do catch fire, the losses will be minimized and fire prevention efforts can be concentrated on this area. At the same time, the other buildings on campus are protected from this fire risk.

Risk spreading is often used for risks that have low probability but would have devastating consequences should they happen. These risks have very high criticality scores and must be dealt with as soon as possible.

Risk Transfer involves moving the financial impact of the potential loss to an insurance company. Although this strategy may seem to be the easiest way for many institutions to deal with risks, it does pose problems. While an institution can purchase insurance to cover payments to victims of rape or murder on campus, these payments can never make up for the criminal act or lost life. Also, the legal liability cannot be passed on totally, and the institution may still be held responsible for negligence or misconduct. Charges of failure to provide a safe environment might also be brought under the provisions of the Occupational Safety and Health Act or the Americans with Disabilities Act.

Finances play another major role in the cost for such insurance. Insurance companies carefully analyze risks to an institution to be able to set a premium rate which will include a profit for them. Rates should be compared among insurance companies and should be renegotiated after any safety or security improvements are made.

Risk transfer is often necessary, however, for those risks that have levels of criticality that are unacceptably high for the institution. Insurance should be used only after the probabilities have been reduced as much as possible using cost effective security and safety measures.

Risk Acceptance is a deliberate managerial decision to assume a potential risk by doing nothing about the threat or setting aside resources that can be used should that threat result in a loss. This risk management technique is not synonymous with merely ignoring the problem. It is adopted only after management carefully considers the advantages and disadvantages of acting or not acting against the threat. Only after that assessment concludes that the risk will not severely affect the institution or endanger the lives of humans should risk acceptance be considered as a management option. This decision is commonly reached when considering smaller risks that have financial consequences only.

For example, the institution might decide to simply replace the few books stolen from the library every month rather than install a state-of-the-art security system for books, which might cost $200,000. By not spending that money on equipment or insurance premiums, the institution might be able to build a nest egg for when it needs money on short notice.

Combination Strategy In reality, no institution is going to adopt just one risk management strategy, but rather will use a combination: Remove and avoid risks whenever possible, reduce and spread the risks of all the others, buy insurance for those risks that cannot be made less critical, and accept those risks the institution can live with.

Cost-Effective Risk Management. Another part of risk management involves handling risk on a cost-benefit basis. Nothing is gained by spending more money for safety and security measures than cost that would be incurred of the loss happened. The only exception to this rule should be when human life is in potential danger. Since life cannot be replaced with money, institutions have an ethical and moral duty to protect all life as effectively as possible.

Risk management is a very powerful tool when used correctly. Administrators at educational institutions should make use of all the variances of the technique to protect their scarce resources—people and money.

About the Author: Dr. Bertus R. Ferreira, CPP, is a criminal justice professor at Washburn University in Topeka, Kansas. Formerly, he was a federal police officer, crime and terrorism investigator, senior security manager, and risk management consultant. He holds six degrees, including a masters of philosophy in policing and crime prevention studies from Cambridge University and a doctorate in occupational and adult education, with a specialization in human resource development, from Oklahoma State University. He is a Certified Protection Professional, Certified Fraud Examiner, Certified Security Trainer, Board Certified Forensic Examiner, Certified Security Executive, and a Life Fellow of the American College of Forensic Examiners.

A member of ASIS, Ferreira has served as a regional vice president and as a member of the ASIS standing committees on academic programs and on educational institutions. He is a frequent presenter at national and international conferences.

Risk Management: A Proactive Program

by Robert C. Nielsen

Throughout my career, I have held various positions in campus administration, beginning at the University of Connecticut, where I served as assistant dean of students and as assistant director of public safety. At the University of Maryland Baltimore Campus (UMBC), I was police chief for nineteen years.

Throughout those years, I was exposed to a fair share of risk management issues, which helped prepare me to take on a newly-created position at UMBC, director of risk management. My staff consisted of an experienced safety officer and a secretary.

Our first task was to determine the scope of the Office of Risk Management. At a recent conference at the Howard Hughes Medical Institute, only two of the twenty-seven schools represented used risk management as a department title. Most of the departments charged with similar responsibilities protect the environment, preserve the health and safety of the campus community, prevent damage to or destruction of campus resources, and identify hazards while ensuring safe conditions and regulatory compliance. Specifically, they deal with such issues as hazardous waste management, laboratory safety, radiation safety, biological safety, occupational safety, emergency response, environmental safety, industrial hygiene, and fire protection.

Defining the task. Had our office been given a more typical title, we might have been able to narrow our focus, but both the administration and the general campus community had great expectations for the new risk management department. As a result, our office oversees such diverse responsibilities as workplace violence programs, worker's compensation claims, lead and asbestos abatement, liability insurance, accident insurance claims and investigations, student health and athletic insurance programs, employee training programs, and air quality inspections.

We share common concerns and objectives with three other departments that also report to the vice president for administrative affairs: the campus police, physical plant, and telecommunications. We assist each other through cross-training, by working in concert during emergencies, and by trouble-shooting campus problems as a team. We not only share equipment, but we also provide each other with information on security and safety problems as well as legal updates

Implementing an Office of Risk Management

College and university administrators preparing to create a risk management department, should take the following steps:

Issue a statement to administrative and management personnel recognizing the importance of safety and accident prevention.

Emphasize to administrative and management personnel that each of them is accountable for creating and maintaining a safe workplace.

Build measurable safety goals and objectives into performance appraisals at various levels.

Establish an appropriate organizational structure to ensure that risk managers have direct access to key administrators.

Develop a specific plan of action for risk management initiatives.

Provide an adequate budget and staff for the risk management department.

Give the department head sufficient authority and administrative support to carry out the unit's mission.

Our philosophy has always been that prevention is much easier, more efficient, and more profitable than dealing with the results of an incident. The campus police devote a good deal of efforts to prevention also. Together, we spent a considerable amount of time on with thefts, burglaries, shoplifting, credit card fraud, bad checks, vehicle accidents, and traffic enforcement, not to mention violent crimes and emergencies of various kinds. Telecommunications oversees the campus phone and alarm systems installation and maintenance.

Achieving the goals. Implementing the programs of the risk management department at UMBD also differs from the norm in a number of important ways. Because of staffing limitations, success often hinges on getting others actively involved in risk management by reinforcing and reminding them of their responsibility for campus safety.

Committees play an important role in promoting and improving campus safety. The Environmental Health and Safety Committee, for example, assists with overseeing and reviewing appropriate health and safety training throughout the university. Chaired by myself, committee members analyze trends, identify safety problems, and make recommendations for corrections. The group assists campus departments with identifying, writing, and implementing safety procedures. This committee has produced several projects, including a seventy-four page laboratory safety manual and two wall charts—one showing waste disposal guidelines and the other on emergency response procedures.

The Risk Management Committee, chaired by the safety officer, assists with preparing and evaluating risk management procedures and updating them as needed. Its members analyze accidents, review safety programs, identify trends, develop corrective measures, and help to prioritize safety projects.

In addition, consultants with certain specialties assist with evaluations, recommendations, and developing regulatory policies and procedures. Within the first year the department's creation, with the help of consultants, policies and guidelines were developed on eleven projects, including radiation safety, hazardous waste disposal, chemical hygiene, work-related injuries, and fires on campus. Wall charts and brochures that spelled out the specifics were prepared to ensure the adequate distribution and dissemination of the information.

Teamwork is key. Those persons who oversee the university's instruction, research, and support services are also the ones who influence and determine the level of health and safety on the campus. As a result, administrative personnel at various organizational levels are encouraged and expected to take precautions to avoid accidents, comply with the safety procedures, and identify potential hazards. An acceptable level of health and safety can be achieved through the teamwork. Each of these individuals is personally responsible and accountable for creating and maintaining a safe work environment. Measurable goals are included in performance appraisals.

The Office of Risk Management assists these persons with safety needs and concerns by helping them to recognize and correct potentially hazardous conditions and practices. To further encourage community input, the risk management department distributes hazardous condition report forms throughout the campus. These reports have alerted us to conditions and circumstances that require our attention. Statistics of on-the-job injuries identify factors that help us make recommendations that will reduce accidents, which can help to lower insurance premiums. One of our goals is to make areas as accident-free as possible by eliminating potential hazards that come to our attention.

Persons who have made a significant contribution to campus safety are recognized through certificates of appreciation issued by our office. A monthly bulletin, "Safety Tips," prepared by our office reinforces our efforts by calling attention to problems and safe practices.

Because perceptions about the role and responsibilities of risk management vary, misunderstandings can occur and must be corrected. Understandably, the Office of Risk Management is often perceived to be the University's primary agent for enforcing safety policies and regulations. But ours is not so much an enforcement function as it is a helping one. Our primary responsibility is to assist administrators, managers, and staff with their safety programs, concerns, and needs.

Support from above. While compliance with federal, state, and local regulations, national safety standards, as well as building and fire codes is important, administrative follow-through is even more crucial. Verbal or written commitments alone don't guarantee a successful risk management program. Key persons have to practice what they preach. Consistent action and participation, not words alone, is necessary if accidents, health risks, injuries, and other losses are to be curtailed. Achieving a safe and healthy campus requires the cooperation of the entire campus community. Conversely, the risk management staff must ensure that key administrators are kept aware of potential risks and problems.

A memo from the UMBC's president to vice presidents, deans, department chairs, and directors urged all employees to comply with established safety procedures and to report potential hazards. The memo observed that, since the establishment of the Office of Risk Management, accident-related leave days were reduced from 237 to 33. The president encouraged persons to contact our office for assistance, noting that we can improve campus health and safety by working together., the campus risk manager must wear many hats and be prepared to deal with countless instances of institutional liability and vulnerability.

However daunting the task may appear, it is far from hopeless. Data collected and hazardous conditions corrected by the unit are of considerable value to the campus. A risk management unit can make a positive contribution toward an institution's success through by anticipating vulnerabilities, identifying liabilities, preventing losses, and preserving campus resources.

After three years, the Office of Risk Management is still developing and determining its role on campus. We continue to discover new and more effective ways to nurture an environment that is sensitive and responsive to the university's health and safety needs.

About the Author: Robert C. Nielsen was named Director of Risk Management at the University of Maryland Baltimore County, Baltimore, MD in 1993, after serving 19 years as the Chief of Police. He is a graduate of the University of Connecticut and the FBI Academy. He has published over 60 articles, has contributed and co-authored books and produced videos on campus security. While serving on the Governor's Executive Advisory Council he chaired the Workplace Violence Advisory Panel. Mr. Nielsen has been named to Who's Who in Law Enforcement, Outstanding Law Enforcement Professional's, Who's Who in the East and Who's Who in America.

Campus Security Act

by Marshall S. Lillie

In 1986 Jeanne Clery, a Lehigh University student, died after being attack in her residence hall room by a former employee of the university. Unfortunately for Lehigh's administration, the old answer of no answer did not placate the young woman's family. Ultimately, their efforts lead to the Crime Awareness and Campus Security Act of 1990, which puts reports on campus crime in the hands of today's prospective college and university students.

In the years since the Act was passed, campus administrators have devised strategies to make the reporting of crimes on their campuses a positive influence on a prospective student's choice while protecting the financial aid status of their institution. That information can help students make knowledgeable choices in their search for a suitable campus environment.

But while the Act may give prospective students some answers, it raises numerous questions for college and university administrators.

What must be reported? The reports must include all criminal acts that occur on campus, which are reported to the administration. The categories of criminal behavior listed in the Act include murder, sex offenses (both forcible and non-forcible), robbery, aggravated assault, burglary, and motor vehicle theft. For easy comparison, these crimes are defined using the same terminology in the FBI's Uniform Crime Report. An interesting statistic that must be included is the crime rate per 1,000 students for each of the categories.

The Act also calls for the publication of the number of campus arrests and complaints for liquor law violations, drug abuse violations, and weapons possession. Institutions are required to report the number of the crimes in each category for the preceding three academic years.

What is a "campus?" The Campus Security Act considers any building or property owned or controlled by the institution as part of its "campus." It also includes any building "reasonably contiguous" to the campus that may be used to support campus activities or the educational purpose of the institution. The definition further encompasses any building or property owned or controlled by an institution-recognized student organization, which may or may not be contiguous to the other campus areas.

The issue raised by this broad definition questions the university's responsibility for reporting illegal behavior occurring at fraternity buildings in which the university has no business interest. In the past, these buildings had been considered "off campus" by the institution, therefore relieving it of any responsibility for the actions of the residents in these buildings. The Act, however, requires the actions of these students to be included in the university's reported criminal activity numbers. The local police are also to notify the college administration of arrests they make at these buildings.

The Act further requires that statistics gathered at each branch campus be reported separately from the statistics of the main campus.

Several attempts have been made to clarify the scope of each report. The State of Pennsylvania, for example, requires that a description of the campus and its boundaries be provided with the report.

What does "reported to the administration" mean? Any valid complaint received by the campus security department must be included in the crime statistics along with incidents reported to the Dean of Students office or similar department. Discussions continue at both the federal and state level about exactly which offices should be required to include data in the annual report. Originally, any report received by a student resident assistant or college counseling center was to be included. Recently, however, counseling centers or administrators with significant counseling duties have been exempted from the reporting requirement. However, any information given to the campus department responsible for compiling the report must be included.

Counselors and counseling administrators were excluded because it is not their responsibility to determine whether a crime took place. Rather, they are asked to report allegations of campus crimes that are made in good faith to the appropriate law enforcement personnel, either campus or local police. If law enforcement personnel, upon further investigation, conclude that the allegations are not substantiated by the facts or the law, the alleged campus crime may be omitted from the statistics.

What else should be included in the report? A statement outlining campus security policies and residence hall security procedures should be included in the report. A description of how the security for campus facilities are accessed and who grants permission for using a facility must also be included. The report must include methods for reporting criminal or suspicious behavior and identify the campus official responsible for receiving and resolving complaints.

In addition, the college or university's alcohol and drug policies must be outlined, along with the addresses and phone numbers of the local alcohol and drug assistance programs. The sexual harassment policy and reporting procedures must be identified, and counseling options available to victims must be detailed. A statement that says victims of a crime on campus may seek confidential counseling and may report the crime to a local police department should also be included.

A description of the authority and jurisdiction of the campus law enforcement agency and its relationship to local police departments must be attached.

Will the statistics be made public? The law requires that security information and crime reports for the three most recent academic years be provided to every employee at the time of hire and then annually thereafter. The report must also be given to all prospective employees, students, or family member who request a copy. All current students must be provided with the report .

In addition, anyone who comes to the campus during normal business hours may view the daily crime log, which is considered to be public information. The daily crime log is a chronological listing of all valid complaints received by the campus law enforcement agency on each day. All felonies, misdemeanors, and summary offenses must be listed. The addresses of the local police departments with jurisdiction over the immediate proximity of the campus should be readily available.

The log must include the complaint number, the time and date received, the classification of the offense, the location of the complaint, the name of the officer who took the report and whether an arrest was made at the time of the report. If any arrest was made, the name and address of those arrested as well as the disposition of the incident must be listed. Laws regarding the privacy of juvenile arrest information still apply, however.

How should criminal acts be reported? The Act requires that the campus community receive "timely notification" of criminal acts occurring on campus. How this notification takes place should be a part of an overall campus emergency plan. Administrators cannot wait until an incident occurs to decide how to handle notification. This decision must be as well thought out as any decision on how to proceed should the campus computer system malfunction.

To reach this conclusion, administrators should determine the likelihood that the incident might pose a threat to others. Based on that assessment, they can then decide how notification should take place, whether through a personal message or through more general warning systems such as bulletin boards or the campus news media. In addition, the person filing a complaint must be advised of its resolution. The result of any campus investigation or action by a sanctioning authority has to be provided to the complaining party.

Should the victim of a sex offense request a change of living or academic environment, the institution must prepare a statement that advises the student that the change will occur as soon as a reasonable alternative is available.

Campus crime is a high profile issue. Parents and students sometimes mistakenly believe that college campuses are crime-free. Administrators cannot allow this misconception to go unchallenged. They must make it clear to their consumers that both students and visitors can come to a campus as predators. Parents and students must also understand that the safety and security of all is partly their responsibility. This conclusion can only be reached through an open discussion about the possibility of victimization and ways to avoid becoming a victim. As institutions that hope to influence students for years after they leave, this lesson may be the most helpful lifelong skill they can learn while on campus.

About the Author: Marshall S. Lillie is currently the Director of Safety and Security at Thiel College, Greenville, PA. He earned a Master of Science degree from Mercyhurst College, Erie, PA. He has been involved in campus security since 1975. He is a member of Northeast Colleges & Universities Security Association and is past president of Western PA College & University Security Association.

Avoiding Liability for Violent Crimes on Campus

by Steve Kaufer, CPP

Premises liability litigation is pervasive in all aspects of American society. Even college and university administrators have been forced to consider this reality when planning and implementing security policies and procedures. Under certain circumstances, for example, state schools can be held liable for victims' injuries resulting from alleged inadequate security, which is outside the boundaries of the governmental immunity usually enjoyed by public institutions or government agencies. Also, students and faculty also expect and demand to be safe where they study, work, and live. As a result, witnesses to campus crimes are usually willing to become involved in a case, since they have a vested interest in its outcome. These witnesses may be frequenting the premises for years, which eliminates a significant barrier to proving a case against property owners.

Until the 1980s, third-party premises liability stemming from violent crime was still an obscure tort action unknown to most businesses and institutions. Today, establishments open to the public have been hit hard, if only through higher insurance premiums, by the specter of potential lawsuits filed by victims of violent crimes. This situation does have a positive side: campus security and law enforcement departments are gradually receiving serious attention and more funding to offset the possibility of litigation

Legislative responses to campus crime. The Crime Awareness and Campus Security Act of 1990 was the federal government's response to the public's growing concern about crimes against college and university students. The act resulted from the 1986 rape and murder of a coed by a fellow student at Lehigh University in Bethlehem, Pennsylvania. The incident sparked a grassroots movement spearheaded by the victim's parents, who initially filed a $25 million lawsuit against the university. The suit alleged that the university had been aware for ten years that students propped open the self-locking exterior doors to residence halls, yet took no action to resolve the problem prior to the girl's murder. The victim's parents and their supporters launched a national media campaign to educate the public about the dangers of campus crime and to push for increased crime prevention and security measures on campuses.

As a result, in 1988 Pennsylvania enacted the College and University Security Information Act (Act 73). Any school that violates that state act can be fined up to $10,000 and be subject to civil action. The act requires all Pennsylvania colleges and universities, including each branch of multi-campus institutions, to provide a report on crime statistics and security measures to students and employees upon request and to notify applicants of the report. They must also provide the Pennsylvania State Police with an annual report of the school's crime statistics for publication in Pennsylvania's Uniform Crime Report (UCR). This annual report must cover the three years immediately prior to its release.

Following the enactment of the Pennsylvania legislation, similar measures were introduced in other states. To minimize inconsistencies in state reporting requirements, a federal bill was introduced and eventually became The Crime Awareness and Campus Security Act of 1990. The act requires that colleges and universities compile and publish annual statistics for the prior years' felonies (UCR Part One crimes), for campus liquor and drug violations, and for possession of weapons violations. The statistics must be provided to the current campus community and to any prospective students and their parents who may request the information. Additionally, each campus must be prepared to present the statistics to the U.S. Department of Education when asked. If an institution fails to comply with the minimal requirements of the act, it can loose its federal funding.

Other provisions of the federal act require that the information in **Exhibit 1** be compiled and made available annually. In addition, campuses must provide information regarding campus sexual assault programs, including programs on sexual assault prevention and awareness; procedures for handling an offense, including on-campus hearings; and policies on informing students of options to notify law enforcement agencies and on notifying students of available assistance.

This well-intended legislation allows students, prospective students, and parents to accurately assess the relative risk of criminal victimization on various campuses. The issue that is not address, however, is that crimes on campus have traditionally been under-reported.

One of the factors leading to students' decisions not to report campus crimes is a perceived lack of effective follow-up by campus security departments. This belief particularly holds true on small to mid-size campuses where security departments may lack the manpower, resources, and training to conduct effective investigations. Students may also perceive a lack of effective discipline for students who are caught; many believe administrations cover for certain students such as highly valued athletes who bring fame and revenue to the college.

EXHIBIT 1

Policies Needed for Selected Provisions of the Crime Awareness and Campus Security Act of 1990

Procedures for reporting crimes or other emergencies, for security and access to facilities, and for campus law enforcement, including the authority of law enforcement personnel and ways the reporting of crimes are encouraged.

The recording of off-campus criminal activity by students through local law enforcement agencies;

Possession, use, and sale of alcoholic beverages and drugs, enforcement of state and federal laws relating to the use of these substances, and drug and alcohol abuse programs available to students.

Administrative response. College, university, and public school administrators—like their private sector counterparts—have given mixed reactions to the increasing concern about campus security. Some have responded with concern and adequate resources; others have viewed the need as a "necessary evil" that cuts into funding for more appealing projects. In those cases, if administrators are face with financial shortfalls, security is often one of the first budgets to be cut.

In other examples, those responsible for security allocations embrace the archaic notion that increasing the visibility of security officers gives a campus the appearance of an armed camp. However, should an incident on campus draw public attention, increased security may be provided for a time, but the status quo returns when the attention dissipates. As many corporations have learned the hard way, a reduction in security manpower or procedures shortly before a violent crime occurs is a plaintiff attorney's dream come true.

The American Council on Education in conjunction with the Association of Independent Colleges and Universities in Massachusetts (AICUM) have long advocated the need for adequate security on college campuses. As early as 1984, the two groups jointly set forth the criteria in **Exhibit 2.** To further underscore security's importance to a solid campus environment, AICUM also recommended that, "institutions need to make their campuses reasonably secure places for all members of their community" by the means listed in **Exhibit 3**. A number of programs can be used to reduce crime on college and university campuses, including the recommendations in **Exhibit 4**.

The foundations of liability. The legal principles of premises liability as applied to specific circumstances vary from state to state according to how each state's appellate case law has evolved. Nonetheless, the basic elements of any finding of liability remains consistent. For such an action to be viable, the defendant must owe a *duty* to the plaintiff, and the plaintiff must have subsequently

EXHIBIT 2

Security Criteria Established by the American Council on Education and the Association of Independent Colleges and Universities in Massachusetts

1. Security must be taken into account in the design, maintenance, and operation of the institution's buildings, grounds, and equipment.
2. Students and other members of the institutional community must be adequately informed about security risks and procedures.
3. Security personnel must be adequately screened, trained, equipped, and supervised by the institution or its contractor;
4. The number of security personnel used must be adequate to perform the functions assigned to the department. If no security personnel are used, the campus should be made reasonably secure by other means.
5. Data regarding security incidents must be collected and receive periodic administrative review.

been injured by the defendant's breach of that duty. For the defendant to owe a duty to the plaintiff, there must be a *special relationship* between the defendant and the plaintiff. In the case of private schools, the contract between the student and the school may create that special relationship.

Some states recognize the doctrine of in loco parentis, meaning that school officials assume a duty to protect a child in the parent's absence. However, this doctrine is more likely to apply to

EXHIBIT 3
Recommendations by the Association of Independent Colleges and Universities in Massachusetts

1. Make an organized effort to maintain an "average degree" of security comparable to that of the surrounding community. Expenditures for security should average 1 percent to 2 percent of the university's total capital and operating budget.
2. Consider restricting access to buildings and grounds.
3. Maintain trimmed shrubbery and adequate lighting.
4. Inform local police of criminal activity through established communications.
5. Maintain a security force equipped with radios, uniforms, and flashlights, are which will be trained, monitored, and disciplined. Its members should have the power of arrest or a way of brining in security personnel with such powers in emergencies. If it is armed, the security force must be qualified annually to carry the weapons and each officer must meet legal requirements. A clear policy must be issued on when the weapons can be used.
6. Use student security patrols supervised by the security department. They should be trained not to confront law breakers, but to summon a security officer or police.
7. Consider an escort service after dark.
8. Restrict access of nonresidents to student housing. The rules can cover visiting hours for the opposite sex, overnight guest rules, rules limiting visitors without a student escort, and rules requiring guests to identify themselves before leaving a reception area.
9. Supervise on-campus and off-campus housing to ensure security. Supervisors should be trained.
10. Lock outer doors to student housing at night, and equip individual residence hall doors and windows with locks. Institutions should have a master key that can be used only by authorized personnel.

schools, camps, or trips for students in the primary or secondary grades. Although courts have heard arguments that colleges and universities act in place of parents, most appellate courts have rejected this theory, holding that college and university students are adults and that educational institutions do not owe that extremely high level of duty of care toward them.

The most common theory behind third-party premises liability lawsuits against colleges and universities holds that the institution undertook a duty to protect invitees by hiring security guards and implementing security procedures but was negligent in performing the security duties it had established.

If a crime was unforeseeable to a reasonable person in the same situation, however, there is no duty owed to an invitee regardless of whether that person is a student, employee, visitor, or trespasser. The courts are continually re-evaluating the level of foreseeability of individual crimes. The foreseeability of a crime has traditionally been a question for a jury to decide but, in an effort to curtail

EXHIBIT 4
Recommendations for Reducing Crime on College Campuses

1. Provide educational programs on alcohol and drug abuse, date and acquaintance rape, and crime prevention in general. The programs should emphasize reporting incidents to local police as well as to campus security.
2. Adopt a policy that states criminal behavior will not be tolerated on campus, and communicate this "zero tolerance" stance to students.
2. Suspend or dismiss students who repeatedly violate alcohol and drug policies.
3. Establish procedures for responding to complaints about security follow up in a timely and appropriate manner. Make note of repeated complaints and problem areas and make certain that they are given special attention.
4. Use outside security consultants to survey and evaluate existing security policies and procedures and to make recommendations. Administrators should be aware that failure to follow up on any recommendation could be used as evidence against the institution in the event of a lawsuit alleging inadequate security.
5. Maintain a highly professional security department, which receives regular training.
6. Use state-of-the-art security hardware such as alarm systems that sound a warning when residence hall doors are propped open. A reputable independent security consultant should be able to make security hardware recommendations appropriate to a particular campus environment.

landowner liability, appellate courts in some states—such as California—have recently suggested that foreseeability should be decided by judges and not by juries.

Increasingly, appellate courts are demanding that the crime be highly foreseeable before the landowner can be held liable for injuries to a crime victim (invitee). This high level of foreseeability can be proven easily if a recent history of similar crimes on the property can be produced. California is among the states that now require a history of similar crimes for another crime to be deemed foreseeable. Georgia uses a requirement for "substantially similar" prior crimes. But attempts at definition often just raises more questions, for example, "How similar is substantially similar?" and "Foreseeable to whom?"

More liberal jurisdictions allow foreseeability to be determined by the totality of the circumstances. By this standard, factors not directly causing the injury but possibly contributing to an environment conducive to crime can be added to the equation. These factors can include lighting, overgrown shrubbery, a history of property crimes, poorly supervised security guards, and the crime rate of the surrounding area. The practice of considering the crime rate of the surrounding community obviously puts urban schools at a disadvantage in defending against these lawsuits. In states such as California, a judicial backlash against using the totality of the circumstances as a standard has developed because of criticism that it places unreasonable demands on landowners to be the "insurers of safety."

In addition to lawsuits alleging negligence in providing security, other lawsuits base their claims on misrepresentation or fraud. This circumstance may occur when the facts are presented inaccurately by the defendant, such as a campus representative telling prospective students that residence halls are crime-free. A lawsuit involving one of those students could allege that the representative 'lulled the plaintiff into a false sense of security." Because of the prevalence of such allegations, most apartment associations now recommend that personnel who used to be called "security guards" now be referred to as "courtesy patrol officers."

Breach of contract actions involving colleges and universities are sometimes based on an admissions or enrollment contract. More commonly, however, they are based on a violation of a provision in a housing contract, usually having to do with lock maintenance or residence hall supervision. These landlord/tenant actions are usually straightforward and thus easier for the plaintiff to prove than the more general allegations of negligent security.

Breach of contract actions based on landlord/tenant law are facilitated in states that recognize an "implied covenant of habitability" for leased residences. This covenant is similar to product liability law: if you buy a product, you have the right to assume it will function for the purpose for which it was bought. Using an implied covenant of habitability defense, a plaintiff can allege that he or she signed a lease with the reasonable expectation of safety from criminal attack while in the leased unit.

Drugs and alcohol on campus. In 1989 Towson State University in Maryland, a campus of approximately 14,000 students, conducted a random survey on crime and its relationship to alcohol or drugs among students. The survey found that perpetrators of violent crimes on that campus were students 70 percent to 80 percent of the time, and that drugs or alcohol played a role in 60 percent to 70 percent those crimes. The same survey indicated that perpetrators are more likely to be freshmen or sophomore male athletes who are in fraternities where members drink more heavily than the rest of the student population.

Assuming the Towson State statistics are typical, about one-third of all campus crime can be directly attributed to students intoxicated by alcohol. Clearly, managing or eliminating the use of drugs and alcohol on campus would very likely have a significant affect on the rate of crime on campus.

While most administrators would endorse that conclusion, they may not be as willing to act accordingly. For example, administrators may avoid adopting an adversarial stance against a fraternity that traditionally fosters alcohol consumption if significant donors to the college are former members of that fraternity. Or administrators may be tempted to look the other way if star athletes who bring revenue and fame to the school also participate in these same fraternities. Selective enforcement can cause resentment among other students, however, and erode respect for both the administration and the rules.

Alcohol education, counseling, and treatment programs should be available both to students who recognize that they have a problem and those who need to be placed involuntarily into such a program. Refusal to participate should result in suspension or dismissal from the institution, and that policy should be enforced. Whenever possible, the school should have its own treatment programs so that the progress of students receiving care can be monitored and evaluated.

Alcohol use and hazing by fraternity members has received increased media attention lately as a result of serious injuries and even deaths. These incidents have prompted most states to ban such behavior, but without strict enforcement by campus administrators and national fraternity offices the behavior can persist. Several alternatives can downplay alcohol consumption during the fraternity selection process. "Dry rushes," where no alcohol is allowed, eliminates participation by students who do so just for the drinking. A deferred rush delays students' ability to join a fraternity until the second semester of their freshman year. Fraternities themselves can sponsor drug and alcohol-free events that promote involvement in community service.

Campus security personnel who are sworn peace officers are obligated to strictly enforce the laws that apply to both underage drinking and illegal drug use. If a clear policy is continually communicated and consistently enforced, it can prevent the situation from getting out of hand

On campuses where drug dealing is strongly suspected or apparent, the security department should team up with local law enforcement officials before considering a drug buy or an arrest. Search and seizure laws must be strictly followed to avoid a civil suit alleging false arrest. Whether a state college or university is immune from such civil liability will depend on the recent case law of that state, but private institutions enjoy no such immunity.

Sexual assaults. In 1986 University of Arizona clinical psychologist Dr. Mary Koss surveyed 3,000 college men and 3,200 college women. The survey was conducted in conjunction with *Ms. Magazine* and was funded by the National Institute for Mental Health.

The survey found that one in five women students had been raped by acquaintances and that one in eight women were victims of rape or attempted rape in the year prior to the study. In addition, 84 percent of the victims of rape or attempted rape knew the perpetrator, and 57 percent of the incidents were "date rapes." Only 5 percent of these rapes were reported to police.

Of the men who participated in the study, one in twelve admitted they had committed acts that met the legal definition of rape or attempted rape. Sixteen percent of that group had participated in gang rapes. In acquaintance rape incidents, about 75 percent of the men and 55 percent of the women had used drugs or alcohol just prior to the assault. Finally, 82 percent of the women who had been victims of sexual assaults reported that the incident had permanently changed them.

A 1985 to1988 study of 1,400 students at a Midwestern university, conducted by Dr. Chris W. Eskridge of the University of Nebraska, produced results very similar to the Koss survey. In this second study, 21 percent of the female students surveyed said that they had been forced to have sexual intercourse. A 1998 study conducted at Stanford University produced even higher percentages. In this study, 33.5 percent of female graduate students and 26.5 percent of female undergraduate students said they had been forced into sexual intercourse.

In the November/December 1993 issue of *Campus Law Enforcement Journal*, Boston attorney Jeffrey A. Newman wrote the following:

> "Date rapes most often occur between two students in the privacy of a room. Unless there was a failure to respond to screams during a rape or instances where the assailant was known by college administrators to have committed similar acts or other violent behaviors, there is probably no liability to the university."

Newman goes on to explain the circumstances under which a college or university could be held liable for a date rape: If a male student has been reported to college or university officials as having raped female students yet little or no disciplinary measures are taken before he rapes again, administrators can be found liable for negligently performing their duty to protect female students from a known danger.

Educational programs concerning rape prevention emphasize swift and effective disciplinary measures for offenders. These steps can reduce the potential liability surrounding these incidents. Campus rape prevention programs should stress the reporting of date and acquaintance rape and convey the message that the campus will not tolerate rape of any kind.

One of the inadequacies of the Campus Crime Awareness Act is that it does not distinguish between crimes among acquaintances and crimes involving strangers, nor does it take into account the degree of violence involved. These oversights can present a misleading picture of campus violence to prospective students and their parents. Remember that detailed reports of all incidents reported must be kept for several years. Should a lawsuit be filed by a rape victim, the victim's attorney will likely attempt to use these statistics as evidence that the institution knew that prior rapes had occurred on campus. The defense attorney, on the other hand, will rely on reports that differentiate between relevant and irrelevant prior incidents.

About the Author: Steve Kaufer, CPP, is nationally recognized for his work in school security and innovative programs designed to reduce the potential for crime and violence in educational institutions. With over 22 years in the security industry, he has developed multi-faceted programs for school districts across the United States. He is the author of several books on school safety. He is a member and vice president of the International Association of Professional Security Consultants, and a member of the American Society for Industrial Security, Association of School Business Officials, Association of Threat Assessment Professionals and the National Association of School Safety and Law Enforcement Officers.

Sample Third-Party Premises Liability Lawsuits Against Colleges and Universities

***Hayes v. State of California,* 521 P.2d 855 (Cal. 1974):** Two young men were assaulted and one was murdered on a beach controlled by the University of California at Santa Barbara. The case was heard before the California Supreme Court, which ruled that governmental entities have no duty to warn against criminal behavior when the public is generally aware of the existence of violent crime in the area. Posting signs warning of crime was held to be an unreasonable duty to impose upon the government. The state was also not liable for maintenance of a dangerous condition since there was no evidence that any defect contributed to the assault.

***Relyea v. State of Florida,* 385 So.2d 1378 (Fla. 1980):** Two young women were abducted while walking to their car in a remote area of Florida Atlantic University during the evening. They were later murdered off campus by the abductor. Survivors of the victims filed lawsuits against the university, alleging inadequate security because the university failed to provide an adequate number of security patrols, provide parking attendants in the area, control access to the university from roadways, and adequately protect persons attending evening classes at the remote site. The Florida Court of Appeals held that the university had no duty to protect in the absence of prior similar acts committed on invitees. No prior violent crimes of any type had occurred on the campus.

***Brown , Substitute Administratrix of the Estate of Whelete Venita Collins v. North Carolina Wesleyan College, Inc.,* 309 S.E.2d 701 (N.C. 1981):** Ms. Collins was abducted from the defendant's parking lot by an intruder on campus, then raped and murdered. The plaintiff filed a lawsuit for negligence on the part of the college. The complaint, which was particularly well-drafted because it hit precisely on the relevant legal issues, alleged that the defendant allowed people that it knew or should have known to have an unsavory character and dangerous propensities to loiter on its campus; knew or should have known the assailant was present on its campus but failed to require him to leave; and failed to adequately light its parking lots and common areas and keep them in a reasonably safe condition.

In addition, the suit claimed the college violated its duty to exercise due care by failing to provide adequate security for its students within its common areas and parking lots and by not protecting its students from foreseeable criminal assaults by third persons in these common areas. The college also violated its duty to warn victim of the dangerous conditions on its campus and violated its own security rules as well as the laws of North Carolina concerning breach of warranty and breach of covenant of quiet enjoyment.

The North Carolina Court of Appeals noted that the North Carolina Supreme Court had, in 1981, established foreseeability of the crime as the standard for determining the extent of a landowner's duty to protect business invitees from criminal assault by third persons. The court examined the issue of foreseeability in the abduction of Ms. Collins and concluded that the only report of a prior violent crime on the campus was an attempted rape three years earlier. The court concluded that this one unrelated prior violent crime was not sufficient to put the college on notice that a crime of the magnitude of the abduction, rape, and murder of Ms. Collins would occur three years later. Without this element of foreseeability, the college could not be held liable.

***Peterson v. San Francisco Community College District,* 36 Cal.3d 799; 685 P.2d 11 93 (Cal. 1984):** Peterson, who was assaulted on a stairway in a campus parking lot, alleged that the college knew of prior similar attacks by assailants who had hidden behind dense foliage on the same stairway. The college had taken steps to increase security in the lot, and the plaintiff stated that she relied on this increased protection. However, she was not warned of the danger when issued a parking permit for the lot.

The California Supreme court agreed that the college had a duty to warn students of the potential danger so that they could exercise more caution, and ruled that the college could be held liable for failing to warn of dangers it knew about. The court further ruled that the college could be held liable for maintaining a dangerous condition by not trimming the shrubbery when they were aware that it had been used as a hiding place for assailants. The school, however, could not be held liable for failing to provide adequate police protection, since it was protected by the state's immunity statute.

This landmark case, liberalized premises liability standards in California until 1993 when the law become more strict [*Note: see* ***Nola M. v. University of Southern California,* 16 Cal.App.4th 421 (1993)**].

***Klobuchar v. Purdue University,* 553 N. E.2d 169 (Ind. 1990):** The estranged husband of the plaintiff entered her car while it was parked in a university parking lot and hid in the back seat under a covering. She only became aware of his presence when he came out from the cover as she was backing up the car. The plaintiff drove off campus, then jumped out of the car and started running. The husband caught her and threw her back in the car. Witnesses alerted the city police who pursued them by car. The husband eventually shot his wife five times, seriously injuring her, then fatally shot himself in front of the police officer.

In her lawsuit against the university, the plaintiff alleged that while the university had a duty to protect her from the criminal acts of third persons, it did not have sufficient security personnel on duty to provide this protection. The Indiana Court of Appeal noted that no facts had been presented to show that the university knew of previous attacks on students in the parking lot or had created a dangerous condition. Therefore, the university could not be held liable for injuries to the plaintiff.

***Crow v. State of California,* 271 Cal. Rptr. 349 (1990):** Crow was attacked and injured by a fellow student during a dormitory party where alcohol was being consumed. The victim sued the state university, alleging that the university had a duty to monitor and supervise dormitory activities and that its failure to do so created a dangerous condition that led to his injury. The case was dismissed by the trial court, and the dismissal was affirmed by the California Court of Appeals. The appellate court noted that the university had no duty to monitor and supervise the party, and that no defect in the dormitory contributed to the injuries. Dismissal was again affirmed.

***Delaney v. University of Houston,* 835 S.W.2d 56 (Tex. Sup. Ct. 1992):** Delaney, a female student at the University of Houston, had reported several times that a key was broken off in the lock of the outside door to the dormitory where she was living. The lock, however, was never repaired. While staying in the dormitory over Easter week, a gunman entered the dormitory through the unlocked door and raped Delaney. She brought a breach of contract and negligence lawsuit against the university, alleging that the university was negligent for failing to repair the lock and provide her with safe housing.

The trial court dismissed the lawsuit on the ground that the university had governmental immunity. The dismissal was affirmed on the same ground by the Texas Court of Appeals. Delaney appealed to the Texas Supreme Court. The higher court held that the university was not immune from liability for two reasons: the rapist was not a government employee or a defendant, and the complaint was based on negligence for failing to repair the lock and not misconduct against the perpetrator of the crime.

This case opened the door in Texas to third-party premises liability cases against governmental entities where the perpetrator is not a government employee who is being sued for misconduct.

***Nola M. v. University of Southern California*, 16 Cal.App.4th 421 (1993):** Nola M. was raped on campus by a man who had apparently hidden in the shrubbery near the campus credit union where she went to make an evening deposit during the Christmas recess. Among other points, Nola alleged that the campus police were insufficiently staffed at the time of the incident and that the university had maintained a dangerous condition by failing to trim the shrubbery. The courts ruled in favor of the plaintiff, and the university appealed based on causation issues.

In its decision, the California Court of Appeals cited *Noble v. Los Angeles Dodgers, Inc.,* 168 Cal.App.3d at p. 918:

> "The present case is a classic example of a plaintiff establishing what could be described as abstract negligence, in the context that the Dodgers' security didn't comport with plaintiffs' experts or the jury's notion of 'adequacy,' but failing to prove any causal connection between that negligence and the injury."

The court pointed out that the university's security officer coverage of the campus was far greater than the Los Angeles Police Department's coverage of the adjacent neighborhoods:

> "... Nola's expert did not, and could not, say that more security guards or guards on foot instead of in cars or lower hedges or more light would have prevented Nola's injuries. And, of course, Nola's expert conveniently ignored the fact that, on the night Nola was attacked, U.S.C. had eight officers patrolling a quarter mile area while the Los Angeles Police Department had about the same number patrolling the surrounding ten and one-half miles.
>
> "... where do we draw the line? How many guards are enough? Ten? Twenty? Two hundred? How much light is sufficient? Are Klieg lights necessary? Are plants of any kind permissible or is U.S.C. to chop down every tree and pull out each bush? Does it matter if the campus looks like a prison? Should everyone entering the campus be searched for weapons?
>
> "To characterize a landowner's failure to deter the wanton, mindless acts of violence of a third person as the "cause" of the victim's injuries is (on these facts) to make the landowner the insurer of the absolute safety of everyone who enters the premises."

The California Court of Appeals thus concluded that the university's failure to deter the attack on Nola was not the cause of her injuries. The case was remanded to the trial court with directions to enter judgment in favor of the university.

[Note: The Nola M. case marked a reversal after approximately ten years of California appellate case law that tended to favor plaintiffs in premises liability actions.]

Wright v. University of Utah, **876 P.2d 380 (Utah 1994):** Wright sued the University of Utah after she was attacked by an autistic employee. The case was dismissed by the trial court, which cited Utah's statutory immunity of government agencies in cases of assault and battery. Wright appealed, claiming that her injuries arose from negligent hiring and supervision of the employee by the university rather than from assault and battery.

The Utah Court of Appeals rejected the argument, holding that a public university is a government function performing an irreplaceable service to the community, and its immune status is constitutional in Utah. The court noted that the plaintiff could not properly argue that she has been left without remedy since she failed to pursue her option to sue the assailant. Dismissal of the case was affirmed.

Johnson v. State of Washington, **894 P.2d 1366 (Wash. Ct. App. 1995):** When the plaintiff was a freshman at Washington State University, she was abducted and raped near her dormitory. The State of Washington was granted summary judgment on the ground that the state, as a government agency, was not liable for breaches of duty toward "the public at large". The trial court also deemed the act of the rapist as the intervening cause of Johnson's injuries.

The Washington Court of Appeals rejected Johnson's argument that the university was acting "in loco parentis" (in place of parents), noting that college students are adults and their attendance at the university was not mandatory. The court found, however, that the university owed Johnson a duty of reasonable care for her personal safety since she was an invitee on campus, required to live in its dormitories, and not a member of "the public at large". The court remanded the case for trial, noting that there were still issues to be resolved, such as whether the university fulfilled its duty and whether the crime was foreseeable.

Emoakemeh v. Southern University, **654 So.2d 474 (La. Ct. App. 1995):** Emoakemeh, who lived in one of the university's dormitories, was injured when a gun held by his dormitory's resident assistant accidentally discharged while the residential assistant was attempting to enforce the university rule that shirts be worn at all times. Emoakemeh was awarded $60,000 damages at the trial court level. The Louisiana Court of Appeals affirmed the award, holding that the resident assistant was attempting to enforce university rules when the shooting occurred. As a result, he was representing the university, making the university partly liable for his misconduct.

Randi W v. Muroc Joint Unified School District **(January 27, 1997) 1997 WL 27555:**

The plaintiff, a thirteen year old girl, was molested by her school's vice principal, Robert Gadams. The ensuing lawsuit alleged that other school districts who had previously employed Gadams wrote letters of recommendation on behalf of Gadams without disclosing the known facts of his history of sexual misconduct. For example, Gadams worked for three years in the Mendota School District, which knew of his sexual misconduct with female students. Despite this knowledge, the district provided a detailed recommendation stating that "I wouldn't hesitate to recommend Mr. Gadams for any position!" The recommendation also set forth various positive aspects of Gadams' tenure.

Gadams had also been employed for two years by the Golden Plaines Unified School District. Golden Plains knew of complaints from parents about "sexual overtures" made to students and that sexual misconduct charges had been brought against Gadams. In fact, Gadams resigned from Golden Plains due to pressure from the school district. Nevertheless, Golden Plains sent a letter of recommendation describing Gadams' "strong points" as a teacher, and stated they "...would recommend him for almost any administrative position he wishes to pursue."

Officials at the Muroc Joint Unified School District provided a letter of recommendation indicating that Gadams was recommended "...for an assistant principalship, or equivalent position without reservation." This statement was made despite knowledge that Gadams had been charged with sexually touching female students, which led to his resignation.

In affirming the Court of Appeals ruling that the plaintiff had indeed stated a cause of action for negligent misrepresentation, the California Supreme Court emphasized the detailed letters provided by the school districts, which affirmatively set forth only positive conclusions and specifically discussed Gadams' personal characteristics. In other words, the fact that the schools knew of Gadams' negative history made the assertions in the letters "misleading half-truths." Moreover, and importantly, all of the school officials knew that their letters of recommendation would be received by prospective employers.

California has traditionally been a bellwether state for legal trends, so it is likely that this new cause of action will likely emerge in other states in the near future. The California Supreme Court in *Randi W* determined that the school districts owed the plaintiff a duty of care but breached that duty of care by making misrepresentations or giving false statements. It further stated that the prospective employer's reliance on the statements proximately caused her injuries. Specifically, the court held:

> "the writer of a letter of recommendation owes to prospective employers and third persons a duty not to misrepresent the facts in describing the qualifications and character of a former employee, if making these misrepresentations would present a substantial, foreseeable risk of physical injury to the prospective employer or third persons. In the absence, however, of resulting physical injury or some special relationship between the parties, the writer of a letter of recommendation should have no duty of care extending to third persons for misrepresentations made concerning former employees. In those cases, the policy favoring free and open communication with prospective employers should prevail."

[Comments on this case were excerpted from "Employer Liability for Letters of Recommendation: To Recommend or not to Recommend?" by Daniel J. Herling, J. D., *Premises Security and Liability.- A Comprehensive Guide from the Experts,* Workplace Violence Research Institute, Laguna Beach, California.]

Controlling Theft on Campus

by Bruce K. Smock

The security and safety problems a college or university differ from those at other business for a number of reasons. The facilities are in almost constant use, and large student and faculty housing units create a virtual city within a city. Even when campuses are located on the periphery of a city, they do not escape the crime problems of the area.

The population density created by the recent trend toward high-rise dormitories has posed new problems in the protection of students and their property. Students living in these dormitories cannot know all the other residents, making it is easier for an intruder to blend in. In addition, college campuses sustain significant losses from the theft of college property, most commonly computers, audiovisual and laboratory equipment, typewriters, calculators, and educational materials. Aside from the liability issues, colleges and universities can suffer adverse publicity and an erosion of public confidence if theft becomes a major problem.

To address these issues, many colleges have installed extensive locking and control systems to restrict access to their buildings, particularly residential housing.

But hardware is only part of the solution. University management, the campus safety director, department managers, and all employees must take responsibility for controlling theft. A number of approaches can be adopted to make the campus community aware of potential losses and control theft on campus.

Becoming aware. The first step in developing a security awareness program involves assessing potential losses in each department, using existing theft records. A security survey can be particularly helpful in completing an exhaustive physical examination of the premises and inspecting all systems and procedures.

The objective is to determine the existing state of security, to locate weaknesses in defenses, to assess the degree of protection required, and to develop recommendations for a total security program.

The survey may be conducted by staff security personnel or by qualified security consultants. Some experts suggest that outside security personnel can provide a more complete appraisal of existing conditions since they might approach the job with more objectivity and be less likely to overlook certain areas or take practices for granted.

In either case, the project needs a strong administrative commitment to achieving results and ultimately providing adequate campus safety and security. This commitment can take many forms, including making sure the campus security director is an integral part of the decision-making process. Most importantly, however, administrative support must include the commitment of sufficient financial resources to the project.

The survey should be structured in three parts: pre-survey surveillance, interviews with department managers, and a summary conference. During the course of the survey, equipment should be inventoried and priorities should be set for protecting various groups of people and assets. Fire safety issues should also be addressed. The type of action needed should an incident occur should be considered. Some possible alternatives include response by security personnel, intervention by security equipment or personnel, or a security hardware deterrent.

From the outside in. The survey should start at the perimeter of the property and work toward the core. To that end, crime statistics should be gathered for the community at large as well as the college or university itself. Fences, lighting, doors, watch towers, and other perimeter barriers should be assessed. Parking lots and other parking facilities should be examined along with campus speed controls and safety patrols. Sound monitoring capabilities as well as closed circuit television installations should be reviewed, particularly if it includes night vision equipment. A similar list of specifics should be developed for surveying internal access controls and departmental procedures.

After potentially high-theft areas have been identified through the survey, appropriate protection systems can be developed. Security components such as closed circuit television cameras, electronic access control devices, door alarm monitoring systems, and intrusion detectors can be used alone or configured into a fully integrated and distributed network. Installing these systems in a college or university setting often involves trade-offs, however. The cost of the installation must be weighed against the cost of the potential losses they will prevent.

The most effective deterrent against theft is an individual's perceived chance of being caught. In places where an opposition to theft is underscored by management and coworkers because these losses are reported, thefts decrease.

If the initial assessment reveals a poor history of loss reporting, developing a program to improve reporting is the first step toward reducing theft. Reports should be routed through one department, and monthly reports should be distributed to all. Each theft should be treated as a serious incident, and a highly visible investigation, where appropriate, should be conducted.

Audits test standards. Another essential component in any loss prevention program is a vigorous internal audit standard. Audits should be conducted in such areas as receiving, supply distribution, and billing and collection. A diligent controller can overlap with physical security by organizing spot-check inspections, checking campus safety officers performance, and verifying the effectiveness of protection measures.

A particularly difficult part of any campus to secure is the parking lot. A combination of good lighting and steady patrolling can reduce parking lot crime, however. If the budget can support it, closed circuit television surveillance should also be installed. The decision on which programs to adopt will depend on the existing lighting and traffic patterns, the number of incidents reported on campus and the surrounding area, and the security departments staffing and monitoring capabilities.

A primary factor in reducing crimes on campus is the employees level of security awareness. Awareness training should be essential for all employees, and should consider the specific security needs of various student, visitor, and employee groups.

For example, employees on the night shift might require escorts to their cars at certain times.

Once an employee awareness program has been developed, participation can be encourage through statements about employee responsibility and behavior in employee handbooks, departmental policies, and procedure manuals. Discussions on security issues and policies at new employee orientation programs, at annual employee in-service programs, and with volunteers and temporary employees should be encouraged. A policy that underscores the need for employees to report all security incidents to a designated campus authority should be disseminated, and those who report or prevent significant criminal activities should be rewarded.

Establishing a sound employee security awareness program, along with a crime prevention program that works in unison with the local police departments community policing program will obviously pay off in the reduction of theft on campus.

About the Author: Bruce K. Smock is presently assigned to the Kettering University Campus Safety Department. He has a Bachelors of Science Degree in Human Services and Criminal Justice Administration. He holds the Advance Law Enforcement Certification from the Michigan Law Enforcement Officers Training Council and the Advance FBI Law Enforcement Training from the Northwest Training Center. He has completed the Healthcare Security/ Safety Officers and Supervisors Certification from the International Association of Healthcare Security and Safety. He has served as an Expert Witness in Security in the States of California, New Mexico, Maryland, Florida and Oklahoma. He has authored and edited numerous articles on Security for the American Hospital Association, the Journal of Healthcare Protection and Management and ECRI in Security and Risk Management Issues for the Control System from the Pennsylvania Insurance Risk Management Company. A Consultant for the Legal Expert Network-Baltimore, Maryland. He has appeared on the Oprah Winfrey Show, Sally Jesse Raphael Show and the Jane Wallace Lifetime Television Show as a Security Exert.

Selected Bibliography:

Bilek, Arthur J., *Private Security* Standards and Goals, *Private Security Task Force.* Cincinnati, Ohio, Anderson Publishing Company, 1977.

Green, Gion, *Introduction to Security.* Boston, Massachusetts, Butterworth Publishers, 1981.

International Foundation for Protection Officers. *Protection Officer Training Manual.* Boston, Massachusetts, Butterworth-Heinemann, 1992.

Post, Richard S. and Schachtsiek, David A., *Security Managers Desk Reference.* Boston, Massachusetts, Butterworth Publishers, 1986.

The Role of Door Hardware in Access Control

by Charles Cameron

To some, the term access control evokes the image of access cards, electronics, and computers. While these technologies are frequently part of an access control system, they are not the sole components needed to make a system complete. Locks, along with the hardware and doors on which they are installed, are an equally important part of a comprehensive access control system.

The physical security of an access control system is frequently evaluated by the type of lock it uses. The mere presence of a lock does not guarantee adequate security, such as when a state-of-the-art electronic reader operates a lock that can be slipped with a credit card or when a lock is installed on a hollow core wood door.

Mechanical Locking Hardware. Mechanical locks have received scrutiny by both standards setting organizations and law makers. Over time, these groups have set requirements on how various types of locks should and can be used. One guide is the American National Standards Institute (ANSI), which sets grades for locking hardware. In their lexicon, Grade I hardware, for example, should be used in situations where durability and resistance to forced entry are most important.

Locking hardware can be divided into two general categories: locksets and exit devices. Locksets are operated by knobs or lever handles that meet the requirements of the Americans with Disabilities Act. Except in very special exceptions, public buildings and campus facilities must have hardware that allows free exit, meaning that the inside knob or lever may not be locked. Life safety codes further require a push bar or pad on exit devices for auditoriums, other large capacity rooms, or doors in a corridor or stairway.

EXHIBIT 1

Types of Locks

Entry: The inside handle is always unlocked. The outside handle is locked or can be unlocked with a push or turn button.
Appropriate for offices, labs and some classrooms.

Classroom: The inside handle is always unlocked. The outside handle is set locked or set unlocked with the key.
Especially applicable in elementary and secondary schools.

Storeroom: The inside handle is always unlocked. The outside handle is always locked. A Only a key allows access, and the door is always locked when closed.
Applicable for mechanical rooms, housekeeping closets, and some storage areas.

Vestibule: The inside handle is always locked. The outside handle can either be locked, or unlocked with a key on the inside. When the outside handle is locked, a key will allow access but will not unlock the outside. The inside and outside cylinders should require different keys.
Applicable when a door needs to be unlocked for public access at times but restricted to key holders at other times.

Dormitory: This strong and durable mortise-style lock has a deadbolt controlled by a key from the outside and by a turn piece on the inside. The inside handle simultaneously retracts the latch and the deadbolt. It require a key to lock the door from the outside.
Applicable in student housing because students cannot lock their key in the room. Also useful in areas that need the added security of a dead bolt.

Exhibit 1 shows the various types of locksets applicable to specific uses in the campus environment.

Mechanical exit devices. Exit devices can be divided further into the following categories: rim, where the lock mechanism and latch bolt are mounted on the surface of door; mortise, where the lock mechanism is fastened into the door; and vertical rod (either rim or mortise), where the locking bolts are at the top and bottom of the door and are operated by rods from the main body.

In general, rim exit devices are fairly easy to adjust, thereby ensuring the security of the opening. Vertical rod exit devices are more difficult to maintain; when out of adjustment, the door can often be opened if shaken. For this reason, pairs of doors are more consistently secure when two rim exit devices are latched to a center mullion.

Exit devices on building entrances are often unlocked by holding the latch bolt in a retracted position with a key or wrench from the inside. When the latch is retracted, the door can simply be pulled open against the holding force of the door closer. Exit devices on stairways and other smoke and fire barriers must be kept closed with a latch. Some exit devices operate much like classroom-, storeroom-, or vestibule-style locksets (see Exhibit 1).

Electronic locks. The first widely used adaptation of electronics to the control of locks was the electric strike. This type of lock retains the mechanical lockset and adds an electrically controlled strike. When the strike is released, the door can be opened without changing any part of the lock itself. The security of the door, then, depends on the proper operation of two pieces of hardware.

Over the years, significant improvements in electronic locks have been made, specifically concerning their versatility, durability, and resistance to tampering or forcing. However, the proper mounting and alignment of the electric strike is still a critical component.

Electromagnetic locks were the next commonly available development in electronic locks. They have become popular as retrofit items that can be surface mounted on the door and frame, thus reducing the amount of skill required to install them. Some concerns have been voiced about their ability to resist forced entry. More significantly, however, they must have power to operate, and if the power is interrupted, the space is unsecured. For this reason electromagnetic locks are not suitable as the primary means of security, especially on perimeter doors.

Recent additions to electronic hardware makes both locksets and exit devices electronic by replacing part of the internal mechanical locking mechanism with an electrically operated miniature solenoid. This type of lock generally is rated highly in performance and operating convenience. Also, should this type of lock malfunction, it can continue to operate as a solely mechanical lock or temporarily be replaced by a comparable mechanical lock until electronic operation can be restored. Electronic hardware can be operated remotely, either for momentary access or for locking and unlocking to meet opening and closing time needs.

When selecting electronic hardware, the concepts of “fail safe” and “fail secure” must be considered. Fail safe means that when power to the lock is interrupted, the lock becomes unlocked and passage is not prevented and therefore safe for exiting. Fail secure means that the electric current keeps the device unlocked and, when current is interrupted, the lock becomes locked and the space is secured.

Electric strikes and electrified locksets are generally available in both fail safe and fail secure modes. Electromagnetic locks are by their nature fail safe. Exit devices are electrically fail secure and mechanically fail safe.

When developing a locking system where security is the priority, the fail secure option is the best choice. In certain situations, however, applicable life safety codes may require that the lock be fail safe. In those cases, the electronic lock should be wired into the fire alarm system and released when an alarm occurs.

Electronic systems. Most people tend to classify electronic access systems by the type of unit that operates it. The most basic unit is the key pad, which requires the user to key in a personal identification number (PIN) or a numerical sequence. The weakness in this type of system is that the code can simply be given to another person or discovered easily. For that reason, key pad systems are not appropriate for high security purposes. They can be used for traffic control in locations where the general public needs to be restricted from access during business hours, but employees must access the area repeatedly throughout the day. Another place where such systems have proven useful is in restricted locker rooms, since a person does not need to be present to control access during the exercise or practice session.

A more secure electronic system uses individual identification. With this system, every user has a unique credential, such as a card or a key, that the lock is programmed to recognize and accept when the user touches it to or inserts it into a reading device. A refinement of this concept is a proximity reader where the credential and reader communicate by radio signals within an operating range. This technology allows the credential to be used while still concealed in a pocket, purse, or book bag. The type of technology used, its durability, and cost vary and will change as improvements are introduced.

Recent developments in electronic access systems incorporate biometrics. This type of system grants access by recognizing a physical characteristic of the user such as the retina, fingerprint, or voice. Biometric systems tend to be expensive and are best suited to facilities where a high level of security is needed, such as research facilities or government projects.

Electronic systems are available as stand alone battery powered units or as units wired to a central controller. In many situations, having a limited number mechanical keys that can bypass the system in an emergency is prudent.

Electronic access systems offer several features not possible with mechanical systems. If a person looses his or her identifier, the lost credential is merely deleted from the system and a new one issued to the user. In a mechanical system, the lock would have to be rekeyed and new keys distributed to all users. With electronic systems, time zones for accepting some, all, or none of the keys can be established. For example, student residence hall entrance keys could be active twenty-four hours a day except during semester breaks, housekeepers keys could work only in their assigned area during specific work hours, or computer laboratories could be accessed by students only during established hours.

Most electronic systems provide an audit trail that record use, which is helpful when investigating problems in a certain area. Finally, persons respect for security increases when an electronic system is used, an intangible benefit but one that may be the most compelling reason to change from mechanical keys.

Mechanical key systems. Mechanical locks used to control access are organized in an interrelated master key system, which uses hierarchical levels of master keys (such as great grand master, area master, building master, and department master) and individual keys, which are controlled by the master keys. A properly designed, maintained, and controlled master key system can be a very effective means of physical security.

A master key system can be implemented in two ways. The first way is to set up a system in response to a critical concern in a specific area. This type of system is inflexible, however, since it cannot be expanded easily. A better approach is to develop a comprehensive facility-wide plan that addresses the unique character and needs of each area of the facility. Once the plan is established, it can be implemented in phases as a critical need arises or resources become available. Also, rekeying a building or department is easier and faster because the information is already available.

A single master key or even the same type or function of lock would not be appropriate for all areas of a university. Building entrances; lecture rooms and classrooms; teaching, computer, or research laboratories; administrative, department, or faculty offices; the bookstore; the pharmacy; and maintenance shops all have specific security requirements that would all need to be addressed on a master key system..

A concern with mechanical key systems is unauthorized duplication of keys. Hardware manufacturers addressed this concern by issuing restricted keyways that are very difficult to duplicate. Eventually, more costly high security keys and cylinders with enhancements to protect against picking and drilling were developed by specialty manufacturers. On university campuses, picking and drilling is as great a concern as unauthorized duplication. Recently, some manufacturers have started producing patented keys and keyways, which can be purchased at a more moderate cost.

Mechanical key systems must be supported by a policy that outlines procedures for issuing, recording, and retrieving keys. A good policy should be brief, should be customized to the university, and should share the responsibility for ensuring the integrity of the system with all users. A sample key policy is shown in **Exhibit 2.**

Avoiding liability. The varied facilities on a university campus have different needs for security hardware and systems. Universities are constantly confronted with the possibility of personal harm or injury to students, employees, and visitors. Security measures must prevent these types of incidents, thereby limiting the universitys liability. As a result, door hardware, particularly in residence halls, must be appropriately monitored and properly maintained.

Other locations where incidents could leave the university liable are athletic facilities, mechanical rooms, and roofs. These areas can be secured through proper keying and key controls as well as self locking locks and automatic door closers. Stairway, corridor, and exit doors are spots of potential liability if the hardware used does not meet life safety code requirements or is not functioning properly.

EXHIBIT 2
Sample Policy for Issuing and Controlling Campus Keys

I. **Purpose:** To protect the assets and property of the campus and associated personal property as well as ensure the physical safety of students, faculty, staff, and guests, the Department of Physical Plant and University Lockshop is responsible for the design, maintenance, and administration of all campus locking systems and associated hardware.

II. **Policy:** An essential part of this responsibility is the control of access to facilities through the selective issue of appropriate keys (keys, cards, codes, etc.) to qualified individuals. Keys to campus facilities are the property of the campus and must be surrendered to the appropriate campus authority upon reassignment, termination, or when otherwise requested. Individuals receiving keys share in the responsibility for the safety and security of the areas accessed by the keys and must, therefore, safeguard the keys assigned to them. Duplication of campus keys is strictly forbidden, and persons obtaining unauthorized duplicate keys are subject to disciplinary action. Lost keys must be reported immediately to the department that authorized their issue, which is responsible for reporting the loss to campus police and the campus lockshop.

A. Lockshop responsibilities:

1. Provide and issue appropriately authorized keys.
2. Receive keys not in active use and provide for their secure storage.
3. Maintain records of all outstanding keys.
4. Advise users on key system structure, capabilities, and status of keys outstanding.
5. Rekey locks to campus standards and specific needs.

B. Departmental responsibilities:

1. Verify and authorize the issuing of keys for their assigned areas.
2. Monitor outstanding keys, collecting those that are not in active use, returning same to the lockshop for safekeeping and future issue.
3. Consult with the lockshop on the status of keying of departmental facilities and newly assigned space to ensure that departmental security and access needs are served.
4. Provide funding for cutting keys and rekeying locks to departmental spaces.

C. Keyholder responsibilities:

1. Safeguard the keys and areas accessed as stated above.
2. Return keys to campus lockshop when no longer in active use.
3. Report any lost keys immediately to department which authorized their issue.

> **III. System design and structure:** Campus policy requires that all campus spaces be accessible by master keys available to campus police and physical plant service employees for performance of their job duties. Additionally, all office and public spaces in buildings must be accessible by master keys designated for the use of housekeeping personnel. In most situations, other users will be issued individual keys specific to the various areas they will be accessing.
>
> **IV. Administration of Policy:** The necessary forms for requesting keys and establishing authorization procedures are available from physical plant. Detailed procedures used to carry out the above policy are on file in the campus lockshop. Consultations with the campus lockshop on specific security questions and needs are encouraged.

Putting it all together. When implementing an overall access control system for a university campus, funding is usually a concern. As a result, the security staff should determine what areas of the campus can be adequately secured with keyed mechanical hardware and which places need an electronic access system. The use of two or more master key systems can be an effective security management strategy. One might use commercially-available keyways while the other may need patented or high security keys that limit the possibility of unauthorized duplicate keys.

Residence halls and office building entrances could be considered for some type of electronic access system that provides an audit trail of use. Other areas may need the added feature of time zones for access by maintenance or housekeeping.

The best way to implement and maintain such a varied array of security system is by employing a person experienced in hardware uses and applications (see **Exhibit 3**). A security professional with a combination of technical and administrative abilities can coordinate and maintain a good physical security system for a university campus.

EXHIBIT 3
Position Description: Manager of Key Systems and Security Hardware

This employee manages the systems and procedures necessary to provide a unified physical security system for a university campus. The Manager of Key Systems and Security Hardware is responsible for the overall function of the various components in the campus physical security system. He/she acts as the liaison between administration and other campus functions in the development and administration of policies and systems necessary to provide security in a planned, efficient, and cost effective manner.

Duties and Responsibilities:

1. Develop and maintain hardware standards and policies to meet the university's security needs through the use of appropriate locks, access control hardware, and builders hardware. Consult with architects and designers to specify hardware consistent with the university's needs and standards. Conduct inspections of hardware installations to ensure that the specified hardware has been installed and functions properly.

2. Develop and maintain a master key and record keeping system to support the access and security needs of the campus. Maintain records of keys and master keys and related rooms by room number and door number. Review and authorize requests for lock changes, installations and rekeying. Direct locksmiths and other trades people in actions necessary to carry out requested tasks.

3. Develop and maintain a key control standard and policy to provide a complete and accurate record of all outstanding keys for university facilities. Review all key requests and authorizations to ensure they conform to policies and procedures.

4. Supervise the specification, purchase, installation, and maintenance of all door and physical security hardware.

5. Ensure that all locks, doors, and door hardware meet the relevant requirements for life safety codes, building codes, and accessibility codes.

6. Act as a resource person or consultant to assist departments in planning and developing solutions to their security issues.

About the Author: Charles Cameron is a Certified Master Locksmith (CML) by the Associated Locksmiths of America. He is currently the Lock Shop Manager at the University of North Carolina at Greensboro, Greensboro, NC. He has 19 years experience as a university locksmith. He has written articles on locks and has instructed classes for the Associated Locksmiths of America. He is a member of the American Society for Industrial Security, the Associated Locksmiths of America and the Institutional Locksmiths Association.

For Further Information

The following professional associations focus on the application and service of hardware used in physical security systems.

Associated Locksmiths of America
3003 Live Oak Street
Dallas, TX 75204
214/827-1701

Door and Hardware Institute
14170 Newbrook Drive
Chantilly, VA 20151
703/222-2010

Institutional Locksmiths Association
PO Box 450
Falls Church, VA 22040
(301) 645-7786

College Bookstores: Retail Loss Prevention Benchmarking

by George J. Okaty, CPP

More than $25 billion in retail sales was lost in 1994 as a result of shoplifting, internal theft, and errors, according to a 1995 survey of retailers conducted by the Security Research Project at the University of Florida in Gainesville. How much of this enormous loss was contributed by your campus bookstore? To ensure that campus bookstore crime prevention programs are effective, retail industry loss prevention standards should be used as a benchmark.

At many universities, campus police or security come in contact with the bookstore only when a suspected shoplifter is caught, a bank escort is requested, guards are needed during busy periods, stolen books are returned, or someone asks for tips on what to do in a robbery. Although these roles are important, other opportunities for interaction exist that will help combat retail loses and significantly add to the universitys bottom line.

Campus security managers need to understand the concept of inventory shrinkage to provide targeted support to bookstore operations. Shrinkage is the difference between the goods received and sold and the goods in inventory. This difference is presented as a percentage of total sales.

For example, a store received 300 shirts and sold 150 shirts. But when the remaining shirts were inventoried, 145 were found on the shelves, meaning five shirts were missing. If the retail value of each shirt was $30, then a loss of $150 occurred. Since the amount received from the sale of the shirts totaled $4,500 (150 x $300), the shrinkage was 3.3 percent ($150 divided by $4,500).

The average shrinkage figure for retailers in 1994 was 1.83 percent of sales. If a campus bookstore brought in $5 million in sales that year, it would have lost more than $91,000 to shoplifting, internal theft, or errors, assuming a shrinkage level of 1.83 percent,.

Of the total losses reported in the 1995 survey, nearly $10 billion was caused by internal theft, $5 billion was the result of administrative errors, and $1.5 billion related to vendor issues. The balance, $9 billion, was attributed to shoplifting. To discover where bookstore losses may be occurring, the security staff should examine four targets: the administrative offices, cash service areas, sales or customer venues, and support locations.

Administrative offices. Administrative offices normally contain the files and computers storing records vital to managing bookstore operations. These records include inventories, merchandise removed from stock, and merchandise transferred from stock. They also contain price, vendor, and accounting records. All of these records are subject to manipulation and can result in massive losses through internal theft or administrative errors. Examples include the creation of false vendor files, the manipulation of deposit receipts, and the improper entry of merchandise received or removed from inventory.

A loss prevention survey of administrative areas should include physical security systems, computer security safeguards, and audit procedures. A system of checks and balances should be in place to ensure no one person has total control.

Cash service areas. Cash service areas include the customer service desk, cash register stations, and the cash office. The customer service desk is especially vulnerable to various types of fraud because it frequently handles customer returns and supports cash register operations. Merchandise being held for a customer or employee is normally stored there, and it frequently functions as the stores lost and found.

Persons working at the customer service desk should be on alert for persons who shoplift with the unsuspecting cooperation of store employees. For example, a customer takes an item of clothing from a rack and brings it directly to the customer service desk to be held, saying he or she is returning it and needs a different size. The thief gets a second article of clothing, returns to the customer service desk, and has the second item bagged for removal from the store. An especially bold thief could even demand a cash refund for the first item. In some cases, employees could be working with others to intentionally commit this type of fraud. To prevent scams of this sort, closed circuit cameras should be used in customer service areas.

Cash register areas are vulnerable to check and credit card fraud, internal theft, customer manipulation, and errors. Examples of internal theft include the intentionally under-ringing of an item or not ringing an item being purchased by a friend or family member. Customer manipulation includes activities such as substituting lower-priced sales tickets on more expensive items. Accidentally handing back too much change to a customer is an example of cashier error. Closed circuit cameras can reduce these types of problems as well.

The cash office is the bookstore bank. It is here that daily operating funds are held, cash register receipts are brought, and bank deposits are prepared. Physical security and good accounting practices need to be closely monitored. An audit trail is important, particularly if financial information is reconciled into a computer. The destruction or alteration of cash transaction records could lead to huge losses.

Customer venues. The third target a loss prevention survey should review is customer venues, including the sales floor, fitting rooms, alteration areas, and rest rooms. Shoplifting is the primary threat in these locations. To combat this threat, security patrols, electronic inventory tags, security mirrors, cameras, and locked display cases should be used as appropriate. However, there is no substitute for customer service as a deterrent to theft. Bookstore employees who frequent customer areas must be trained on how to prevent shoplifting before it occurs.

Studies of shoplifters indicate that about 75 percent of those caught are average citizens who steal for personal use and have no criminal record. An additional 20 percent have a criminal record but still steal for personal use. Professional shoplifters, unusually two or more people working together who steal regularly to resell merchandise, make up about only about 5 percent of those caught.

Several issues should be considered in developing a shoplifting training program for bookstore sales staff. The program should stress greeting the customer and being available to monitor the customer's actions. If detaining a customer is a store policy, it should be implemented only when an employee directly observes a subject obtaining possession of an item and concealing it. Should an employee detain a customer who went into a rest room or fitting room with an item but exited without it, such an act can lead to litigation if the customer left the item in the fitting room or rest room. Employing fitting room attendants or requiring customers to leave merchandise outside of the rest room can avoid costly legal battles.

Another training goal is to teach bookstore staff how to deal with a suspected shoplifter legally when initiating an investigation. Not all states have clear shoplifting or merchant's privilege statutes. In Texas, for example, the Civil Practice and Remedies Code permits a retailer to detain someone to investigate ownership of property, not to arrest. The use of force or accusations early in an inquiry can be disastrous. The inquiry should also be completed in a legally reasonable time.

Bookstore employees should clearly understand the legal difference between what they can do under probable cause and what campus police and security authorities can do. If store management doesn't have enough evidence to prosecute before a police officer is called, the incident could lead to a law suit even if the original inquiry was legal.

Support locations. The final target for review by campus authorities is bookstore support locations such as employee break rooms, lockers, storage closets, trash receptacles, and shipping and receiving operation. The opportunity for internal theft is especially high in employee areas. Trash receptacles should be inspected for merchandise dumped there so it can be picked up later. Employee lockers can be used to store items that could exit the store inside of handbags or backpacks. Routine inspections of employee lockers, backpacks, and handbags should be considered. Key control policies should be closely examined.

A loss prevention review should pay particular attention to the shipping and receiving operation. Not only is this area vulnerable to vendor theft and employee theft, it is also vulnerable to paperwork errors that could result in thousands of dollars in losses. Accepting the wrong number of cartons in a shipment or placing the wrong number of cartons on a transfer form for shipping can increase losses.

Typically, the receiving area is used to prepare and tag merchandise before it is transferred to the sales floor. Physical security concerns, procedural controls, and audit trails should be included in all shipping and receiving operations. Receiving doors and dock areas should be locked when not in use. Logs should be maintained when outside doors are used and when merchandise is received and sent out. The use of CCTV cameras and alarm systems should be considered as well. Incoming stock that is transferred to the sales floor should always be checked against the purchase order to ensure that an error has not been made in the quantity or pricing of the merchandise received.

Understanding where loses can occur in bookstore operations is the first step toward reducing shrinkage. For a commercial retail operation, the difference between a shrinkage rate of 3 percent and 1.5 percent could stave off bankruptcy. In a campus environment, the difference means dollars saved for the benefit of students and faculty. Campus crime prevention and loss prevention efforts can make a difference in preserving dollars earmarked for education.

About the Author: George J. Okaty, CPP, is a past chair of the ASIS Educational Institutions Standing Committee, was the Director of Security and Safety at the Delaware County Community College in Media, PA and was the Director of Security and Safety at Trinity University in San Antonio, TX. He was also an adjunct faculty member at the Delaware County Community College and was a teaching associate at the University of Texas at San Antonio. He is an experienced retail Loss Prevention Manager, having worked for the Stein Mart retail chain. Mr. Okaty has a Masters Degree in Public Administration and is a security management consultant. He is currently the Security Manager for the McNay Art Museum in San Antonio, TX.

Managing and Preventing Gang Activity on Campus

by Kenneth S. Trump

Gangs? Not on our campus! After all, gang members don't go to college.

Although this school of thought may have accurately applied to campuses of the 1950s, today's progressive administrators must recognize that gangs, like all other societal groups, have no boundaries. Just as violence, drugs, weapons, and other safety and security threats that were unheard of in most secondary and primary schools several decades ago, today they are commonplace, and so are gangs. How should higher education administrators react?

Alarmed? No.

Aware? Yes.

Concerned and proactive? Absolutely.

One of the most important steps in successfully preventing and managing gang activity on any campus is recognizing its current or future presence. By far, the majority of campuses across the nation are not overrun with gang members. However, the potential presence and, in turn, potential activity of gang members continues to grow.

Individuals, organizations, and communities, in their efforts to recognize and respond to gang violence, can adopt any one of the positions described in the accompanying "Gang Awareness Continuum." Administrators who take a balanced and rational approach to gang issues have the best chance to effectively manage both the problem and the public attention it engenders. However, administrators who embrace one of the first three positions are likely to contribute to the problem instead of effectively managing it. Likewise, overreacting and taking extreme measures will also result in management and public controversies.

Recognizing gang identifiers. Identifying a gang member or gang activity was once a relatively easy task, but is becoming more difficult since the signs are more subtle. The following list includes some of the more common identifiers.

Graffiti: Gang members have traditionally marked their "turf" with the signs, symbols, and names of their gangs as well as their individual monikers on buildings, walls, desks, tables, chairs, lockers, phone booths, bulletin boards, and cafeteria tables or any other spot they encounter. Gang members, particularly in secondary and elementary schools, often carry gang literature (or "lit") in and on their school notebooks and even label their textbooks and homework assignments with specific gang symbols.

Colors: Initially, individual gangs adopted certain colors, which were displayed on such items as clothing and bandannas. Today's gangster, however, may be much more low keyed, identifying themselves with only a subtle piece of jewelry, a particular brand of clothing, or a unique hairstyle.

Tattoos, hand signs, handshake: Gang members may display signs of their gang affiliation as tattoos on their arms, chest, hands, or other locations on the body. They may also use a particular hand sign or handshake associated with their gang. "Stacking," the rapid display of multiple gang hand signs, is another common identifier.

Initiations: To join a gang, potential members are often required to be "beaten in" or "jumped in" by multiple members. What may appear as an assault to an unknowing bystander may actually be a voluntary gang initiation. Numerous unexplained bruises or suspicious injuries on a student's body may the result of a gang initiation and may warrant further attention.

Increased awareness of these identifiers by educators, law enforcement authorities, parents, and community leaders has resulted in the decreased use of blatant colors, signs, and symbols by gang members. Instead, they often adopt a lower profile, leading educators to mistakenly believe there is no gang presence.

Potential affect. Gangs can affect a campus environment in a variety of ways. The following prevention and response measures can be used to deal with the effect of gangs.

Graffiti and vandalism: Campus law enforcement officers, administrators, and maintenance crews should be trained to recognize gang graffiti and to report these observations to their security department. Photos should be taken of the graffiti, and it should be removed quickly and consistently.

Auto theft: Parking areas on and adjacent to campuses should be patrolled and monitored regularly. Gang members may steal cars simply for a joy ride, or they may intend to resell the parts to obtain cash. While campuses generally are not singled out as a primary target for auto theft, they do provide an opportunity for gangs who have access and an interest in exploiting auto thefts.

Robberies, assaults, and property thefts: Gang members, like other criminals, prey on easy targets, be they persons or property. A strong campus crime prevention program that includes awareness training on reducing behaviors conducive to personal victimization will help reduce risk. Bookstores, high-value equipment areas such as computer rooms and media storage areas, and similar campus sites should be secured and monitored by professional security staff.

Drugs: Gangs are often involved in a significant amount of drug trafficking. Campus officials, while handling traditional drug-related campus crimes, should keep in mind that this new breed of players may be involved. While the propensity for violence in drug cases is high in general, it can be even higher when gang members are involved. All drug incidents should be consistently reported, thoroughly investigated, and aggressively prosecuted.

Athletic and social events: Gang members, like other students, like to hang out and have fun. Campus officials should be aware of the potential for gang members to be present at athletic events, dorm parties, or similar activities.

Some gang-related violence stems from personal conflicts, romantic jealousies, or rumors. Unlike one-on-one conflicts, however, gang-related offenses hold a greater potential for violence to escalate, because they can include a large number of participants and weapons. Security, police, and campus administrators should keep these facts in mind when responding to conflicts and altercations.

Some gangs are attempting to legitimize their organizations by claiming to have shed illegal practices and adopted community improvement programs. Some gang members have even attempted to run for political office. While certainly former gang members can change, colleges and universities, in the tradition of scholarly debate and research, could easily be targeted by gangs whose reform rhetoric only covers continued criminal endeavors.

All campus rules and regulations should be enforced in a firm, fair, and consistent manner. Special event planning should include adequate staff that can handle large scale or violent disruptions. Details, such as the event's sponsor, specific activities, and anticipated crowds, should be gathered well in advance by campus security staff. The safety of all, including those individuals responsible for providing security services, should be a priority.

Personnel security: Contrary to popular stereotypes, gang members do hold traditional jobs. In fact, some gang members have even applied for security and police positions. All applicants for jobs at a college or university should undergo criminal history checks and thorough background investigations to determine their suitability for employment.

Computer and technical equipment: Obviously, valuable equipment should be adequately secured. The use of the equipment, however, should also be monitored. Secondary and even elementary school students, including gang members, have used school computers to produce counterfeit money, obtain formulas for making bombs, and create "gangsta" Internet web pages. Campus administrators should establish, publicize, and enforce "acceptable use" policies for all school computers and other technical equipment.

Awareness and training. Like any criminal organization, potential gang activity is only limited by the creativity of its members. Campus administrators must aggressively participate in ongoing awareness programs and proactively adopt prevention measures that focus on gangs and their specific security threats.

Realistically, however, these actions can present public image concerns for many educational administrators. If they publicly dealing with gang issues, they fear the public will perceive that their campus is gang-infested and thus not an appropriate place to send their children. While these concerns are valid, they must not outweigh actions intended to maintain campus safety. If the potential problem of gangs is ignored, negative publicity nightmares could become reality.

Image concerns can largely be addressed through proper education and training. Campus administrators, instructors, support staff, students, and community members as well as campus law enforcement personnel should participate in gang awareness sessions.

School officials can help reduce potentially negative publicity by preparing before incidents occur. Administrators should send a clear and consistent message that their attention to potential gang activity is based on the desire to maintain a safe and secure educational setting.

Gang Awareness Continuum

Lack of awareness: No one develops an understanding of gangs, and authorities cannot address a gang problem once it arises.

Denial: Authorities recognize that the problem exists elsewhere and may know an appropriate response but refuse to admit that the problem exists locally.

Qualified admittance: The problem is recognized and confronted in only in a limited manner.

Balanced and rational approach: A comprehensive strategy that incorporates prevention, intervention, and enforcement is used to manage gang members and their activities.

Overreaction: Often fueled by high-profile incidents or negative publicity, the problem is perceived to be greater than it actually is and the response is equally distorted.

In addition, administrators should encourage staff to play a role in the broader community's response to gangs. Academic experts can link their research to practical gang prevention, intervention, and enforcement activities, for example. College educators can help develop and evaluate the community's gang prevention, intervention, and enforcement efforts. The campus can host conferences, training, and continuing education classes geared to increasing awareness of gangs and violence prevention. Campus security officials should network with other law enforcement agencies, professional organizations, and community groups to maintain updated information on gang and other local security threats.

Colleges should also integrate gang violence and related subjects into their core criminal justice, education, and social service curriculum. Many educators enter teaching or administrative jobs with little exposure at the undergraduate or graduate level to gangs, drugs, weapons, or violence. It is no surprise, then, that these professionals find it difficult to deal with these problems in their classrooms.

Today, our colleges and universities are not overrun by gangs, and there is no reason to assume they ever will be. Campus administrators who take a proactive but balanced and rational stance will help to ensure that this assumption does not change.

About the Author: Kenneth S. Trump is President and CEO of National School Safety and Security Services, a Cleveland-based national school security and public safety consulting firm. He has over 15 years of front-line experience in urban and suburban school security as a school officer, investigator, gang unit supervisor, director, and national consultant. Ken served as assistant director of the federal-funded Tri-City Task Force Comprehensive Gang Initiative for three Cleveland (Ohio) suburbs, where he also was the director of safety and security for the ninth largest Ohio school system. Prior to those positions, he served over seven years with the Cleveland Public Schools' Division of Safety and Security, where he designed and supervised its nationally-recognized Youth Gang Unit. Since 1989, Ken has also consulted and trained in 30 states and in Canada on youth violence, gangs, and school security. He provides frequent interviews and background consultation for local, national, and international media, including Good Morning America, ABC World News Tonight, NBC Nightly News, CNN Headline News, CNN Talk Back Live, the Associated Press, The L.A. Times, The New York Times and numerous other print, radio and television organizations.

Reference

Trump, K.S. (1996). Youth gangs and school safety. In A.M. Hoffman (Ed.), *Schools, violence, and society.* Westport, CT: Praeger.